UNEARTHING

NEVERMORE

A COLLECTION OF GOLDEN SHOVEL POETRY

INSPIRED BY EDGAR ALLAN POE

TRISHA LEIGH SHUFELT

Copyright February 2024

© Text and Art by Trisha Leigh Shufelt-All Rights Reserved

Cover Art-Trisha Leigh Shufelt

Book Design-Trisha Leigh Shufelt

Copy Editor-Candice Louisa Daquin

Edgar Allan Poe text and quotes-Public Domain

Art images-1st published with Schiffer Publishing/Red Feather MBS-

ISBN-13: 978076436251-the Poe Tarot-December 2021

Alone-Previously published in Sunder the Silence by Trisha Leigh Shufelt-9/2023-

ISBN-9798987748466

Imprint- Trisha Leigh Shufelt Art in Soul, MA, USA.

First Printing-February 2024

ISBN-9798987748473

PRAISE FOR UNEARTHING NEVERMORE

"Whether you are a fan of gothic poetry, Edgar Allan Poe or Golden Shovel poetry as a form, you will discover in Unearthing Nevermore, a plethora of incredibly well-honed writing and sumptuous interpretive artwork. This accomplished collection is devoted to Poe's vision, and utilizes the echoing refrain of Golden Shovel poetry, to exact a flawless homage to Poe's dark voice. But there is so much more; not simply paying tribute to Poe and her love of his work, Shufelt is in her own right an outstanding poet and artist, who puts more into a small book of poetry than many accomplish in a lifetime. Her uncanny skill as writer, is well suited to the Golden Shovel artform, whereby she seamlessly evokes Poe's velvety shadows, alongside her own vision of his world. To be able to compose a poem that is exacting and executed with such precision and imaginative flare, whilst adhering to the rules of Golden Shovel, is remarkable. Shufelt is a master of this form, elevating it as she tightropes through Poe's landscape with her own glorious words. An outstanding achievement, impossible to match, Shufelt has done it again. If you weren't already half in love with her pulsating radiant world, you soon will be."
Candice Louisa Daquin, Senior Editor, Indie Blu(e) Publishing /
Associate Editor, Raw Earth Ink.

"Shufelt immerses the reader "Beyond the Veil" crossing generations, genres, and genius. Her poetry enhances the perceptions, unleashing the sixth sense we rarely use; the imagery from the words combined with the visuals from the art intensifies the reading experience, knowing Poe lives within these pages."
Carmen Bouldin & Jeanie Smith-The Six Degrees of Edgar Allan
Poe/Poe Unplugged Podcast

"An excellent book of poetry that cleverly infuses Poe's lines into new pieces. Shufelt not only utilizes Poe's genius but pays homage to it with her own poetic ability. Her illustrations are a captivating bonus."
Levi L. Leland-Creator, owner, and administrator
edgarallanpoeri.com & A Walking Tour of Poe's Providence

"Fans of Poe won't be disappointed by this inspired collection. Plus, Trisha Shufelt's heartfelt lines might just have you writing your own 'golden shovel' poetry."
Catherine Baab-Muguira-Author of Poe for Your Problems

3

Unearthing

Nevermore

A Collection of Golden Shovel Poetry

Inspired by

Edgar Allan Poe

Art in Soul

I would define, in brief, the poetry of words as

the rhythmical creation of beauty.

Edgar Allan Poe

The Poetic Principle-1850

To my beloved, Andrew

AUTHOR NOTES
WHAT IS GOLDEN SHOVEL POETRY?

Like many poets, I go through dry spells and look for ways to shake things up. I pulled out my collection of Diane Lockward Poetry workshop books, which I highly recommend, and came across a prompt for writing Golden Shovel poetry. I'd never heard of the contemporary poetry form created by Terrance Hayes and was intrigued. Actually, I was mystified. It stirred my creative juices, and I've been a fan ever since. For those unfamiliar, Golden Shovel poetry uses a line(s) from another poem (a poet you wish to honor) to form the end word in each line, and when joined together, it refers to the inspired author's original work. I wrote a handful of GS poems for my book *Sunder the Silence*, but as many of you know, I am a massive fan of Edgar Allan Poe. I knew it was only a matter of time before I wrote an entire GS book dedicated to his brilliant words. I've included illustrations originally featured in the Poe Tarot, published by RedFeatherMBS. I hope you enjoy my deep dive into this phenomenal poetic form, and if you are a poet, I encourage you to drag out your shovel and start digging. You won't regret it.

Trisha Leigh

Contents

NEVERMORE

Wounded words, **once**
spoken, gave me no token and washed like waves **upon**
my misguided memories. **A**
sodden, silent stillness ticked away the **midnight**
darkness as pantomimes plagued my **dreary**
fallacies. Portentous was its suddenness; **while**
unable to stifle the sickness, **I**
stood upon life's precipice and **pondered.**
Tremulous and **weak,**
I could no longer speak **and**
realized the years I had squandered. Too **weary**
from phantom failures and **over-**
played strictures, I abjured my woeful plight. **Many**
moments shattered and replaced the battered in **a**
few eloquent written words that night. **Quaint,**
yet potent the paint, covered my pendulous thoughts. **And**
tamed my pain through its simple reframe. *How **curious***
and wonderful, I thought. At last, my internal **volume**
was silenced, and the dirges of
hope that melancholy burden bore were long-**forgotten.**
I found this and more hidden in the pages of dusty **lore.**

The Raven 1845

A Malstrom of Muses

Oh, how **they**
tempt me. Melodious muses **who**
captivate my senses, dare me to **dream**
impossible dreams, and melt me in madness **by**
their presence night and **day.**
Who dares ignore their wanton whispers? We **are**
merely pawns in their chess game, **cognizant**
only of the insatiable desire to please and not **of**
the damnation behind our drive to deliver. **Many**
see them as succubus **things.**
I see them as lamenting lovers longing for a time, **which**
we cannot measure. Do not dissuade with delusion. **Escape**
is futile. In fact, I willingly choose **those**
haunted lovers **who**
dare me to **dream.**
If **only**
I could live forever and write poetry in their honor **by**
the light of the stars upon the inky black **night.**

Eleonora 1842

"It is a happiness to wonder;
It is a happiness to dream."

Morella
1835

ALONE

is not lonely. Alone is freedom **from**
unwanted company. From my **childhood's**
beginnings until I come to my final **hour**
I will welcome my alone time. **I**
would rather retreat into solitude and **have**
my thoughts be my soul companion than **not**
be alone but lonely with others. That, I've **been.**
Some will do anything to avoid being alone, **as**
though the time spent with the self and not **others**
would awaken who they don't want to be. **Were**
I deprived my precious alone time; **I**
believe I would have lost much. I would **have**
lost luminous hours of enlightenment, **not**
seized the strength of my spirit, nor **seen**
my creativity climb from beyond its depths **as**
I emerged from your well, renewed. While **others**
court companions, I cherished you. I **saw**
what others could not because **I**
listened to your stories. I **could**
not ignore your need to be seen. I could **not**
ignore your need for reclusion, nor fail to **bring**
myself to the shores of your silence. **My**
poetry is tied to your **passions**
like *Calliope* calling me home. **From**
the moment you cried out to me, **a**
bond formed between us; a **common**
thread bound us, and a **spring**
of love flowed within us. **From**
it, all loneliness disappeared. From **the**
moment we merged; we became the **same**
source-
The mystery which binds me still, **I**
will never solve, nor **have**
I the desire. I have **not**

18

the will to leave you lonely. I've **taken**
all I need from the outside world. **My**
world belongs to you. There is no **sorrow**—
I've left that in the company of strangers, **I**
once called friends. I **could**
never return to their falsities. **Not**
an inch would I give to spare them space. I **awaken**
filled with you by **my**
side and in my **heart.**
We, two, need never be lonely. We choose **to**
discover **joy.**
We choose to never look back **at**
the lonesome road before we became, *We*, or **the**
sanity we sacrificed for some **same**
sad need for approval. No **tone**
need ever be hushed when alone, **and**
we no longer need be alone. **All**
is well when we are alone that **I**
am certain. For I have **lov'd**
being alone and **I**
am **lov'd**
alone.

THE WEIGHT OF WOE

The ignominy of my thoughts drift **and**
rift within me **so**
that I am at war with my core. My very **being**
is bellicose, but I am tired. I am no longer **young**.
I am no longer unburdened, **and**
it seems time has **dipt**
me in doubt. My true self has awakened **in**
how my thoughtless cadence, my **folly**,
cultivated the weight I now carry. I
am rancorous within the walls of my ramparts. I **fell**
into the misery of my making. I swam **in**
depths of loathing when I should have shown **love**,
and now, all I am left **with**
is the rotting fruit of my moldering **melancholy**.

Romance 1829

21

All The World's A Stage

I've often wondered if this life is
a cosmic hat containing all
our dominant thoughts. Are we
weaving its threads into what we see?
Are we wearing our illusions as a collective, or
have we Hatters gone mad? While it may seem
that life is a game of chance— a
role of the dice. Perhaps Fate controls the dream.
She's a magician manifesting the madness, and within
her matrix, our *misery is manifold*, revealed through a
trick where nothing exists but the illusion of her dream.

A Dream Within a Dream 1849
Berenice 1835

23

"Just as the day dawns to the friendless and houseless beggar who roams the streets throughout the long desolate winter night—just so tardily—just so wearily—just so cheerily came back the light of the Soul to me."

The Premature Burial
1844

THE GRAY GHOST

I find I cannot grieve **but,**
instead, gather **the**
grains of glass from within the broken **void**
and swallow the shards. The sharp stains bleed **within**
my splintered soul, yet I cannot purge the sins of **my**
resistance and ignite Lacrimosa's song within my **heart.**
I am the gray ghost I've **refused**
to free. I find contentment in the unconventional, **even**
though I should feel malaise in such madness. **Thus,**
I shall embrace the shadows if only **to**
embody the emptiness that consumes everything. I'll **be**
the silent specter whose heart refuses to be **filled.**

Eleonora 1842

27

The Devil Is In The Details

Pins prick pensive perceptions. What does one **believe**
when stasis overshadows sense? **Nothing**
eases the dis-ease that snakes inside **you.**
No words of comfort can console you when all you **hear**
is your heart thrumming in your ears, **and**
every escape evaporates before your eyes. If **only**
the fear that mantles you like a bird of prey were **one,**
you could tame. Yet you feel split in **half**
by the desire to drown and the brawn to breach **that**
invisible surface that holds **you**
bound to the devil you can't **see.**

The System of Dr. Tarr and Prof. Fether 1845

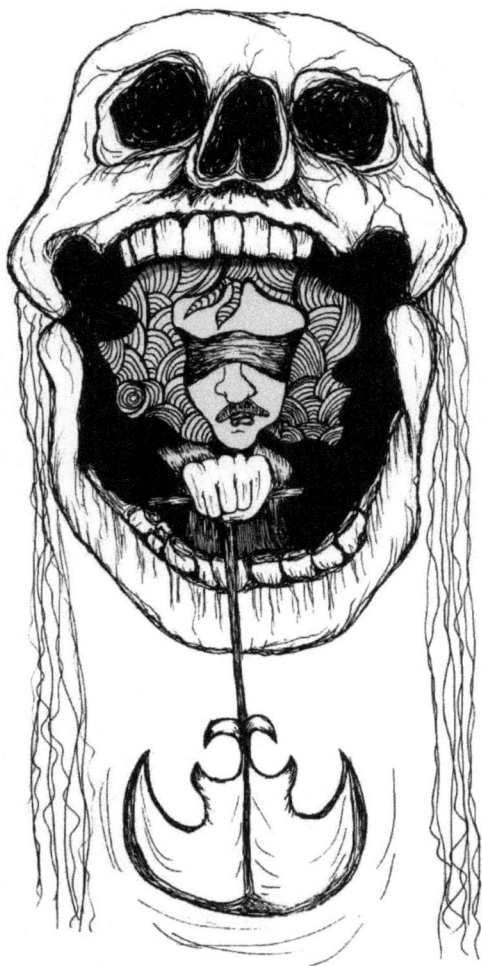

"A wrong is unredressed when retribution overtakes its redresser. It is equally unrepressed when the avenger fails to make himself felt as such to him who has done the wrong."

The Cask of Amontillado
1846

THE BELL TOLLS FOR ME

But lo, the seraphs seek retribution. **Resignedly,**
my resistance yields to their unearthly power **from**
which my internal demons distract. I bend **beneath**
the weight of their wrath as though **the**
stars were stones thrown from the heavenly **sky.**
I can no longer turn a blind eye to **the**
part I've played in your demise or my **melancholy**
disguise, which now drowns me in its wicked **waters.**
No redress can deny or surcease the iniquitous **lie.**

City in the Sea 1845

THE MAGIC OF WORDS

What if our words were spells we
cast, whispers we **gave**
weight without worry, writings wished upon **the**
stars who, through divine alchemy, coalesced a **future**
where all our dreams come true? We dare **to**
dream and imagine but believe **the**
impossible isn't probable. We cast doubt to the **winds.**
Yet the winds are listening, **and**
the moon watches in her glow. What if we **slumbered**
in peaceful reassurance and **tranquility,**
believed the unseen was in magical motion, and trusted **in**
our abilities to conjure resplendent results? Oh, **the**
mystery of manifestation is **present**
and alive, **weaving**
wonderful worlds into **the**
unknown, waking **dull**
moments—a **world**
of pure magic is **around**
us, flowing and ebbing within **us.**
If only we could step beyond what we see and **into**
the possibility of our **dreams**

The Mystery of Marie Roget 1842

"It will be found, in fact, that the ingenious are always fanciful, and the truly imaginative never otherwise than analytic."

Murders in the Rue Morgue
1841

A Thief In The Night

The hourglass turns, and
I close my eyes. *Now*
is the winter of my discontent. I was
afraid to face it, yet once acknowledged,
I knew who I was but knew not what I might be. The
irony of awakened truth, all from a foreign presence
that planted itself like a seed of
rue in my right breast. And with it, the
dark night of my soul unmasked itself, and the Red
Devil poured me a drink of Death.
"This will kill everything inside you except one thing," he
said. Nothing before had
prepared me for what was to come.
And I absorbed the claret wine like
it was the blood of Christ mixed with a
dash of Death himself. Together, we would best the thief
who had stolen pieces of my soul, and in
return, I would become the
light in the journey of my darkest night.

The Masque of the Red Death 1850

A Toast To A Lie

We circled **around**
the subject, sailing **by**
years of **lifting**
silt, shaped by watershed **winds**.
We purged our polluted protestations and **forgot**
what salt can do to a wound. We **resignedly**
made our indifference indelible, but **beneath**
the surface, **the**
bitter barnacles blistered, and the **sky**
wept with our loaded lesions. **The**
stilted silence siphoned **melancholy**
from our stagnant shallow **waters**
and served us a poisoned **lie.**

City in the Sea 1831

41

"But the raven, sitting lonely on the placid bust,
spoke only that one word, as if his soul in that
one word he did outpour."

The Raven
1845

THE TALE I LONG TO TELL

A feeling for which I have no name floats the breeze. It
releases an unease that **is**
familiar and **impossible**
to relent. Perhaps it harkens back **to**
a childhood imprint. I cannot **say.**
Yet now, it haunts me night and day. It shakes me **how**
the feet **first**
met the edge of my spine and sped **the**
bony staircase to my mind, invoking an insatiable **idea**
I can only entertain as insane. It **entered**
as a momentary ideation, but now the *demon in my*
view binds my **brain,**
and from *ev'ry depth of good and ill* is **but**
madness instilled. A thought I **once**
admonished, but now, I must be honest. I **conceived**
it without drink or delirium. **It**
was always a festering bacterium. The vulture **haunted**
my every waking moment and confronts **me**
now. Today will be the **day**
I close his pale blue eye from my sight, **and**
these thoughts that plague me shall vanish with the **night.**

The Tell-Tale Heart 1843
MS. Found in a Bottle 1833
Alone 1829

Bedlam Bells

Delusions aside, I wondered **how**
long it will be before **the**
echoing emptiness entombed me. **Danger**
can be a subtle snare in sanity's reeds that **sinks**
one slowly into madness **and,**
without warning, **swells**
into an all-consuming abyss. **By**
the Gods, I wish I had paid attention to **the**
warning bells. Now, I am **sinking**
into shadow. **Or,**
I have become **the**
shadow itself, a darkling, **swelling**
and swallowing every morose metaphor **in**
its path. I am **the**
hollow girl, harvested in **anger**—
a cold iron bell around the neck **of**
a ghost. I am the abulic aftermath of **the**
warning bedlam **bells.**

The Bells 1848

47

"There is no passion in nature so demonically impatient, as that of him who, shuddering upon the edge of a precipice, thus mediates a Plunge."

The Imp of the Perverse
1845

WINTER'S DISCONTENT

I am lost in the winter of words I
penned from a pale rook's quill. I **became**
perched on the edge of **insane**
reasoning, haunted by ghosts **with**
whom I share shadows as **long**
as forgotten lore. And between **intervals**
of sleep and awake, I peck puzzle pieces **of**
poetry from the frozen ground as the **horrible**
din of silent snow swallows my **sanity.**

From a letter to George W. Eveleth 1848

51

THE SLOW DECLINE

began in **her**
eyes. A **gentle**
sigh of a curtain closing. Her **life**
retreated into the remnants of a dream. Yet, death **declined**
to deliver her still. Instead, she ebbed away **like**
a dusty memory edged in **shadows.**
All I could do was watch **in**
silence as **the**
woman I loved faded like a **dying**
rose. While she was spared the burden **of**
my loss, it seemed time held no mercy for me as **the**
sickness stole her away, and the seconds ticked the **day.**

Morella 1835

53

"Lord, help my poor soul."

Edgar Allan Poe's last words~10/3/1849

Writer's Block

Silence grew fat like a worm feasting on honeyed fruit. I let
it favor my flesh until its meal made a home in **my**
mind and **heart**—
Fear and doubt will **be**
the seeds that sprout and **still**
the flow of poetry through my pen. **A**
vine only time can tame but a teaching **moment**
in the surrender **and**
refrain. **This**
silence isn't a **mystery**
but a moment my muse needs to **explore.**

The Raven 1845

BEYOND THE VEIL

I close my eyes, only for
a moment, and the
sleep comes. Moon
magic and never-
ending stories woven from beams
of starlight wonder. I fly without
fear into the abstract abyss, bringing
poetry and paintings back with me
that can only be imagined in my dreams.

Annabel Lee 1849

"For the most wild yet most homely narrative which I am about to pen I neither expect nor solicit belief."

The Black Cat
1845

Hush My Love

Time watched as **we**
danced in the warm glow of youth. We **called**
down the thunder and rolled **it**
between sweat-soaked sheets until **the**
passion in our veins became a **river**
carrying us along the current of
life. Our fingers separated into the **silence**
that stilled our rushing river's roar. **For**
a while, I stretched here, and you moved **there.**
And it **seemed**
the distance would be **to**
no one's benefit. It would **be**
what damned us. But then, **a**
benefic breakthrough—**hushing**
and gentle in its **influence**
        moved the river. **In**
time, a bridge between **its**
        well-worn banks allowed love to **flow.**

Eleonora 1842

Spirits Of The Dead

Oh, these thoughts that intervene **thy**
conscious hours and stir thy **soul**
from its peaceful bower **shall**
call the void from the highest tower, and ye shall **find**
the urge to jump is in **itself**
a dispatch from the *spirits of the dead*. Who **alone**
would dare dismiss 'mid
earthly gifts that such bliss exists beyond the **dark**
matter of dreadful death? Are the nature of these **thoughts**
a malady of the mind that exists because **of**
some delusional dalliance? *Something* calls in **the**
lonely silence, pervades the **gray**
stillness, and shalt not vanish until beyond the **tombstone**.

Spirits of the Dead 182

65

"I was never really insane except upon occasions
when my heart was touched."

Letter to Mrs. Marie Clemm
1849

AN ODE TO POE *(Morella 1835/The Raven 1845*

I sat **there**
in the sylvan silence; a whisper **was**
heard. The autumn leaves stirred as **a**
caw cried out from the throat of a corvid bird. In the **dim,**
dreary shadows, a figure emerged from the **mist.**
An unkindness of ravens echoed his name and flew **over**
the trees that reaved the sky of its steely stars. "All
hail the Master," they cried as feathers fell from **the**
sky and inky blackness covered the **earth**
in a cloak that celebrated his triumphant rebirth. **And**
as the last feather turned into **a**
silver quill, all the cold, all his earthly ills became **warm**
and seeded the leafy ground with an infinite **glow,**
never to diminish, only to grow. His name **upon**
the lips of every poet in **the**
land, across the **waters,**
and within every hourglass sand. Now **and**
evermore, the Master shall take his flight **amid**
dreams that loom the crescent night. He shall inspire **the**
poor and the **rich**
with his words and rhymes. This **October**
7th, 1849, *weep now or nevermore.* He **leaves**
a legacy extending to the banks **of**
every shore. *Be still. Let this mystery explore.* For **the**
winds wish him well, as do every **forest**
creature who dwells within the ancient realms. **A**
bell rings within the deep well of his resonant **rainbow**
ridge—a sepulcher **from**
which his words still live, and ravens fly between **the**
heavenly **firmament**
and death's darkened edge. He **had**
come and departed solemn just as **surely**
as the last dew-drop autumn leaf had **fallen.**

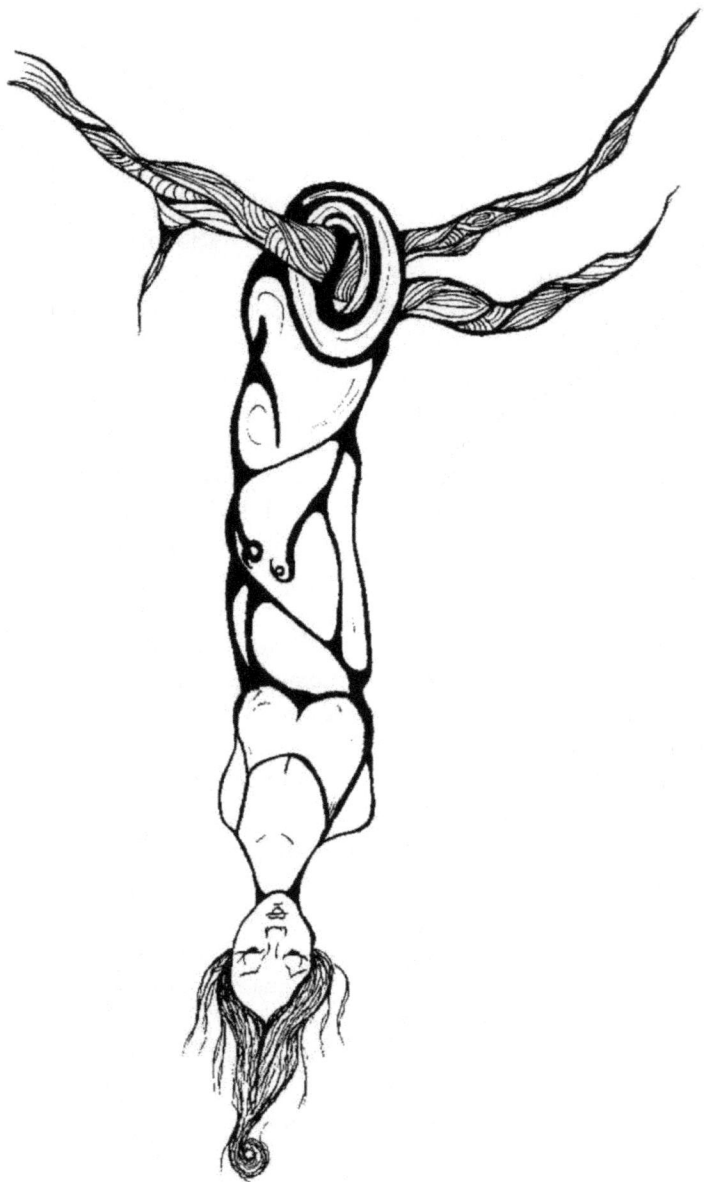

Bones To Butterflies

Humans cannot face **what**
the trees understand. *Shrouds have no pockets.* **We**
barter our lurid truths when death comes to **call**
while the trees release their gilded colors in a **death**
dance like brittle bones breaking into butterflies. Death **is**
a specular secret written within the veins of each leaf **but**
only revealed in the silence leaning to listen after **the**
branches break free of their **painful**
fears and glide with grace into their **metamorphosis.**

Mesmeric Revelation 1842

71

The Black Cat

E A Poe

"Upon my touching him, he immediately arose, purred loudly, rubbed against my hand, and appeared delighted with my notice. This, then, was the very creature of which I was in search."

The Black Cat
1845

The Weight of Wine

Eight ounces in my right hand. I
take a drink. Now, seven remain. I intend
to finish the entire glass, which will lead to
another where the weight of contents will not be put
in my belly but in my thoughts—up
where eight ounces feel like eight tons. And with
it, others will join the party, fat and loathing with nothing
left to lose except Sanity. That
lithe lady left long ago, and I
imagine she is happier now that she can
surface above the contents that only put
anchors on her to pull her down.

Letter to J. Beauchamp Jones 1839

Mirror, Mirror, On The Wall

When did it happen? **And**
why did she **let**
herself disappear? Was it **the**
imposition of servitude that led to the **burial**
of self, a swallowed sacred **rite,**
or an expectation of what others wanted her to **be?**
The mirror didn't lie, nor did the shadows that **read**
like an epitaph on her face. Each line told **the**
stories leading up to her **funeral**—
each dark circle was a **song**
played with an endless skip. She longed to **be**
the wreck that broke the cord of songs **sung**
in the key of pain—**a**
force to be reckoned with instead of the lifeless **dirge**
on repeat between her ears. Where **for**
art thou? Where did you go? **The**
time has come to break the mirror and, **most**
importantly, bury the shards between the **lovely**
and the lost. A place where the **dead**
can remain, and you can blossom anew. **That**
is where you'll find her, **ever**
longing to leave what **died**
in the reflection of someone **so**
old behind a face so **young.**

Lenore 1831

"The question is not yet settled whether madness
is or is not the loftiest intelligence."

Eleonora
1842

A MYSTERY OF MYSTERIES

Although my thoughts are cumbrous **now,**
snared in a stalemate where the wild wraiths **are—**
Although my **thoughts**
tread in slack water. I shall not sink. I know **thou**
art wicked. You **shalt**
not mute this swan. Thou shalt **not**
cover me in your sullen shroud nor **banish**
me to bedlam's abyss. I see thee **now.**
Phantoms feeding on false fears! Thou **are**
baleful **visions**
bleeding me of my sanity. Leave and **ne'er**
return! Scatter your irreverence, blather **to**
the wind, and **vanish**
from my thoughts! Please! **From**
the depths of my marrow, leave! No? **Thy**
purpose is not morose, you say? **Spirit,**
I hear thee, now. These phantoms—**they**
have stories to tell, and they wish to **pass**
them on through me? Then, **no**
harm to me if I am but a vessel. **More**
ease, please, and I shall pen their woes upon the world **like**
a mad poet. And from the melancholy **dew-drop**
my ink shall flow **from**
the depths of my soul until silent, and in **the**
solitude may I find everlasting peace neith the **grass.**

Spirits of the Dead 1827

SELF-PORTRAIT

Rag and bone. I
am. A pointillism painting, I became.
Made **insane**
by the image painted **with**
broken brushes. I **long**
for the realm between the **intervals**
of light and dark where a painting **of**
dots doesn't reveal a **horrible**
picture I am forced to hang on the walls of my **sanity.**

Letter to George W. Eveleth 1848

"I stand amid the roar
Of the surf-tormented shore,
And I hold within my hand
Grains of the golden sand."

A Dream within a Dream
1849

Now She Lays You Down To Sleep

Your words sunder the silence, **arousing**
my somnolent muse **from**
her sepulcher. Like Lazarus, she rises from **the**
ashes aflame with the **most**
resplendent moths starved for **profound**
pearls **of**
poetry only found within surrendered **slumbers.**
When we believe **we**
are empty, she is there to **break**
the glass that separates us from **the**
hidden realms and gather its **gossamer**
spider's **web,**
weaving threads **of**
magic into ink born of **some**
decadent **dream.**

The Pit and the Pendulum 1842

87

Moonlit Musings

Wind-scattered leaves are nature's poetry **for**
the wandering poet whose shadow shines by **the**
light of the **moon**.
It quickens the pulse to witness the **never—**
ending golden pages turn under her pearlescent **beams**.
A poet who pens upon her parchment knows **without**
her, their ink would sink, **bringing**
madness to their melancholy. For **me**,
I shall sit in silent awe and awaken to her **dreams**.

Annabel Lee 1849

89

"And think that these weak lines are written by him—By him who, as he pens them, thrills to think his spirit is communing with the angels."

To Marie Louise (Shew)
1848

THE AWAKENING

Long **after**
our demise, Time will remember **the**
memories of our voluptuous dreams that **lapse**
between reality and fantasy like a pendulum. **Of**
those precious **sixty**
seconds and **minutes,**
will there be a moment that **came**
before death where all that we've known **yet**
denied becomes clear? Will we be given **another**
chance to course correct, or will the **chiming**
echo ring for an eternity in the ears **of**
the ignorant until all that is left is **the**
remnants of a broken **clock.**

The Masque of the Red Death 1850

Memento Mori

I've long contemplated **the**
date of my demise. **Boundaries**
between life and death, **which**
we are all called to cross—An inevitable **divide**
date danced upon in the bristling of **life**
we fail to feel. Omnipresent, Death is with us **from**
infancy until the flesh's final fabric falls. **Death**
is a constant companion, courting us until we **are**
one with her sister, Fate, **at**
which time, there are no bargains to bear. No **best**
efforts shall avoid her **shadowy**
sermon as you pen your name in her book **and**
she writes the final death date—a **vague**
day in your waking life, but now an epiphany. **Who**
shan't see their crossings without awe? Who **shall**
dismiss the times Death touched them unaware and **say**
they were not blessed to live another day? **Where**
were they, and what were they doing? **The**
moment is lost on no **one.**
Still, nothing **ends**
despite the date. **And**
those precious passings, **where**
we were blithely unaware, will be **the**
day our **other**
life **begins.**

The Premature Burial 1844

FOREVERMORE

Each line, each word he quoth
still echoes in the
blood of every raven
whose caw cries nevermore.

The Raven 1845

"Oh! That my young life were a lasting dream!!"

Dreams
1827

Sources & Appreciation

There are many sources out there on Edgar Allan Poe.
Some of the places used for quotes and reference are as
follows-

www.poemuseum.org
www.poeinbaltimore.org
www.poestories.com
www.poetryfoundation.org
www.poets.org
Entertaining reference points -
www.sixdegreesofpoe.com
www. beyondtheoblongbox.buzzsprout.com
www.facebook.com/virtualpoetoaster

A big thank you to-

Carmen & Jeanie of the Six Degrees of Poe for all your
support.
Catherine Baab-Muguira-Author of Poe for your
Problems-your kind words and support mean the world to
me.
Levi Lionel Leland-my friend in Poe. I am so grateful for
your words.
My copy editor, friend, and fellow poet Candice Louisa
Daquin-you continually inspire me.
My family-for your unwavering love and support,
especially my husband (my coffee fairy and partner in
rhyme).

About the Author

Trisha Leigh Shufelt is an award-winning artist, author, and poet.

Poetry Works Include
Liminal Lines- Poetry & Prose
Liminal Lessons- Poetry & Prose
Break & Bloom-Poetry & Prose
The Ghosts of Nevermore-Poetry, Prose & Short Stories inspired by the works of Edgar Allan Poe-A 2023 Saturday Visiter Award Winner through the Poe House & Museum of Baltimore, MD.
The Ghosts of Winterbourne-Poetry & Prose
Sunder the Silence-Poetry & Prose

Poetry & Short Story Anthology Works Include
Evermore-Raven's Quoth Press
300 South Street Publishing-
Love is Helpless
Immortal Tales
Shadow of the Soul

Published under the pen Andaleigh Archer include-
The Underwood Wicked Fairytale Series
Underwood-A Wicked Beginning
Thorn Apple-A Wicked Spell
Quietus-A Wicked Ending
Maeve-A Wicked Beginning
The Promise ~A Faerie's Tale
Red Cinder Swan

Artist & Author works through Schiffer Publishing/RedFeatherMBS include-
The Poe Tarot- Nominated for a 2022 Saturday Visiter Award through the Poe House & Museum of Baltimore, MD & winner of a Bronze 2022 COVR Visionary Award.
The Everglow Divination System

Other works include-
Passion for Poetry-A poetry review journal for poets and poetry lovers

You can find out more about Trisha at
www.trishaleighpoetry.com